BRITAIN IN OLD PHOTOGRAPHS

AROUND
EAST GRINSTEAD

DAVID GOULD

SUTTON PUBLISHING LIMITED

Sutton Publishing Limited
Phoenix Mill · Thrupp · Stroud
Gloucestershire · GL5 2BU

First published 1997

Cover photographs: *front*: J.C. Finch, the
muffin man, in the 1920s; *back*: East Grinstead
Bowling Club, 1913.

British Library Cataloguing in Publication Data
A catalogue record for this book is available from the
British Library.

ISBN 0-7509-1356-8

Typeset in 10/12 Perpetua.
Typesetting and origination by
Sutton Publishing Limited.
Printed in Great Britain by
Ebenezer Baylis, Worcester.

East Grinstead Town Museum was established in 1976 through an initiative by the East Grinstead Society. It was able to draw on three main sources of artefacts and photographs, notably those collected by a former vicar and displayed in the church tower. Its area of acquisition now centres on the town of East Grinstead and its former parish (which once included the village of Forest Row) and any nearby villages which do not have museums of their own. These are all represented within this volume.

The museum is run entirely by volunteers and relies for its income on the sale of publications and donations from the public. It is also generously supported by the East Grinstead Town Council, which allows the museum to use part of their premises at East Court for a peppercorn rent.

There are over 5,000 photographs in the museum's possession. These outnumber the artefacts but among the latter are items dating from the medieval period, when East Grinstead was an important and thriving market town, and a fine display of pottery rescued from the now, sadly, defunct East Grinstead pottery.

The museum is open on Wednesdays and Saturdays from 2 p.m. to 4 p.m. and there is no charge for admission. I hope that this book will encourage those of you who have not yet made a visit to do so in the not too distant future. You will be most welcome!

Dorothy Hatswell,
Hon. Curator.

CONTENTS

Band Sergeant William Harding, 5th Sussex Rifle Volunteers, 1864. The *East Grinstead Observer* described him as a 'fairly good musician' but it was as a photographer that he was best known. He died in 1922 aged eighty-four. (William Harding)

INTRODUCTION

In this second selection of past views of East Grinstead we also explore the villages that lie within a few miles of the town. The photographs show some areas of Ashurst Wood, Coleman's Hatch, Copthorne, Crawley Down, Dormansland, Felbridge, Forest Row, Hammerwood, Hartfield, Lingfield, Sharpthorne, Turners Hill, West Hoathly and Worth. There are 202 illustrations, of which East Grinstead has the lion's share – seventy-four – as befits its importance as a large town.

The coverage of each of the villages cannot be comprehensive, and some places are given greater precedence than others. This is mainly because of the availability of good pictures; in making our selection we had to reject several unsuitable views such as poorly printed original postcards (which do not reproduce well) and street scenes utterly devoid of life (which could well be excellent photographs technically, but make dull pictures). As for such subjects as churches and brass bands, we have selected representative pictures only, so that, for example, Coleman's Hatch and Worth churches are included, but those of East Grinstead and West Hoathly are not.

Most of the East Grinstead pictures have not been published for at least thirty-five years, and some never before. Quite a few have been selected from a vast collection of Edwardian postcards gathered by the celebrated local journalist and historian, Wallace Henry Hills. On his death in 1932 they passed to Brian Desmond, another local journalist who was keen to keep the past alive. After he died in 1995 the collection came to East Grinstead Town Museum.

East Grinstead, a north-Sussex town, 30 miles from London by rail and by road, stands at an altitude of about 450 ft above sea level. The name, originally Grenestede, means green place or clearing in the Forest of the Weald. The town itself was founded in about 1230 and was known variously as Grenestede or Est-grenested, as was the parish. The pictures show the town in the days when it had its own Member of Parliament, its own Urban District Council, a cattle market, a police court, brickworks and a gasworks. Now, it has none of these things, while other recent losses have included the West Street Cricket Ground and the Playfield (although many other open spaces do survive).

South-east of the town is Ashurst Wood – 'Ash-wooded Hill Wood' – which is about 400 ft above sea level. In 1164 it was Foresta de Essehurst, but did not become a significant place until the nineteenth century. Continuing south-east we come to Forest Row, about 225 ft above sea level. This became a place where noblemen built houses to stay in while they were hunting on Ashdown Forest. The next village on our tour is Hartfield (200 ft above sea level), named as the open place where deer were kept.

Now we turn to Surrey for a look at Dormansland, Lingfield and Felbridge, all of which lie north of East Grinstead. Dormansland, formerly a part of Lingfield, became a separate ecclesiastical parish in 1884. The name refers to land held by the Deremans (Deremannslond) in the fourteenth and fifteenth centuries. The present village, whose name is sometimes rendered as Dormans Land, is mainly a nineteenth-century creation and stands about 350 ft above sea level. Lingfield's earliest known reference is in about 875. This village stands on a sandstone hill about 200 ft above sea level, and the two main parts, around the church (Old Town) and the pond (Plaistow Street), were not joined until the nineteenth century. Felbridge, whose name first appeared as Feltbruge in the twelfth century and means 'bridge by the open land', is about 300 ft above sea level, and Felbridge Water marks the boundary between Surrey and Sussex on the present A22 road. The site of the London–Brighton Roman road passes just west of Felbridge.

Worth is a large parish that included Copthorne, made a separate ecclesiastical parish in 1881 with the church of St John; Crawley Down, a separate ecclesiastical parish from 1862; and Turners Hill, a separate ecclesiastical parish in 1895 with the church of St Leonard. Worth itself has the magnificent Saxon church of St Nicholas. Crawley Down was first mentioned in 1274, and the name means 'the hill near the pasture where the crows gather'. The village itself, however, dates from the late nineteenth century.

To the south-west of East Grinstead are the twin villages of West Hoathly and Sharpthorne. West Hoathly – Hadlega, Hodlega (eleventh century); Hodleigh (fourteenth century); Hothelegh (sixteenth century) – stands 600 ft above sea level, and from a certain point nearby one can see both the North and South Downs. There is a disagreement as to the correct pronunciation of the village's name: 'Hoath-lee' is favoured by traditionalists but 'Hoath-lye' is gaining ground among incomers. As for Sharpthorne, it seems that the last syllable should be stressed. This village is almost entirely late nineteenth-century, and stands 475 ft above sea level.

Most of the photographs in this book are from old picture postcards some being the work of national publishers such as F. Frith & Co., many others by local publishers such as Arthur Harding. A few are believed to have been produced by photographic agencies for exclusive sale at the village post offices or general stores, whose names appeared on the card. Whatever the source, it is hoped that this selection of photographs of East Grinstead and its surrounding villages will prove of interest and give pleasure.

EAST GRINSTEAD STREETS

Middle Row as seen from the Parish Church tower, looking south, c. 1905. At the left-hand end is the shop of W.J.S. Mann, tailor, and at No. 5 (right) that of Arthur Wood, piano dealer.

High Street looking west from the corner of Cantelupe Road, *c.* 1920. A conversation is being held outside W. Branson's shoe shop, 'The Golden Boot'. Just discernible is a large wooden boot over the shop blind; it now hangs outside Russell & Bromley's shop in London Road.

High Street, east end looking west, showing on the left the expertly reconstructed Cromwell House after the fire of 1928. This view appears to date from the mid-1930s and the old Rose & Crown (replaced by the present structure in 1939) is seen on the right. (Tooth's Art Series)

A.F. Bettridge's carts posed in the High Street early one morning, *c.* 1919. Bettridge's firm undertook general delivery work in East Grinstead for several years. Second from the left is Ernest George Leppard ('Old Chike'). On the extreme right is his son George Ernest ('Young Chike'), aged about sixteen, who was not an employee but had been called in to hold the horse. The other two men have not been identified. (A. Harding)

South side of the High Street, with part of the back of Middle Row to the right, 1953. The Wilmington Bookshop, at Wilmington House, later moved across to the north side of the High Street at Nos 55/57. Broadley Bros, seen here further along at Nos 38/40, was established in 1896. (E.A. Sweetman & Son Ltd)

A charming view of the shops and brick path on the south side of the High Street, 1949/50. Shop fronts visible include 'Knit & Sew', Tyler & Co. wine merchants, and E. Tooth stationers. The lime trees were planted in 1871 (not 1874 as previously thought). (Valentine & Sons Ltd)

Edwin Tooth's stationer's shop, the fifteenth-century Tudor House on the south side of the High Street, 1952. The shopfront and oak bark decoration date from about 1880. Note the display of picture postcards (mouth-watering to a present-day collector) and the splendid 'Horsham slabs' on the roof. (E.A. Sweetman & Son Ltd)

Interior of F. & E. Tooth's shop, *c.* 1905. The shop was known as F. & E. Tooth's until 1923, when it became simply E. Tooth's. The extraordinary array of items for sale includes books, picture postcards, stationery and artist's colours. (W. Page)

The coronation of Edward VII is celebrated in grand style in East Grinstead High Street, 9 August 1902. In the centre of the picture the orphans from St Margaret's Convent are seen with banners. (W. Page)

The coronation of George V, 22 June 1911. In the High Street the 5th Royal Sussex Rifle Volunteers are performing a *feu de joie* to mark the occasion, and, in the left background, the Military and Town Band is playing. (A. Harding)

An occasion of great solemnity in the High Street, *c*. 1910. This funeral is thought to be that of a military personage; leading the bier, bound for Queen's Road Cemetery, is the top-hatted undertaker Frank Brinkhurst, of Henfield Villa, Cranston Road. (East Grinstead Photo Co.)

The west end of the High Street from the bank at the end of Middle Row, 1959. A London Transport green 'RF' type bus on service 434 from Crawley to Edenbridge picks up a good load of passengers, while the presence of a new three-wheeled car helps to date the picture. (Valentine)

Judges Terrace and its most impressive feature, Clarendon House, 1952. It was built in about 1500 and its timber framing was revealed in 1939. The Clarendon Restaurant was closed in 1968 and the house became offices. (E.A. Sweetman & Son Ltd)

Adjoining Clarendon House is Old Stone House, the older part of which dates back to the early seventeenth century. This early 1930s view shows the late nineteenth-century westward extension (right). On the extreme left of the picture are the former ironworks of G. Woolgar, finally demolished in 1965. (Wiseman Horner)

London Road from Rock Gardens (where the Whitehall now stands), looking south. This unusual view was obtained by using a telephoto lens. On the left is the Grosvenor Hall; at the top Constitutional Buildings; and on the right A.W. Norman's builders' yard. (A. Harding)

London Road, north of the Queen's Road entry, 1883. The shops on the west side still exist – although very much altered – but the elms on the east side no longer exist, having been removed to make way for more shops. (W. Page)

London Road, with the building occupied by the *East Grinstead Observer* from 1894 to 1981 on the right, 1909. The structure itself dates from 1891, the work of the local builder Edward Steer. The fine clock on the Institute building (left) has, since 1955, been fixed to a specially built tower some distance north on London Road. (Kingsway Series)

Looking north along London Road from Constitutional Buildings, 1959. Since then only the Swan (left) and the Placeland water tower (seen against the sky) have disappeared. Heading north is an 'RT' bus on route 409 from Forest Row to West Croydon; this service ran daily with departures at twenty-one minutes past each hour from both termini. (Valentine)

Queueing in the rain for a sale at C.M. Wilson's drapery store in London Road, *c.* 1904. When Wilson's later expanded their frontage right up to the Queen's Road junction they took over the grocery shop, Reeves, which moved across the road to No. 39. Wilson's flourished from 1887 to June 1965. (A. Harding)

William Taylor & Son, furniture and art dealer, at 208 (later 218) London Road, *c.* 1905, having just moved there from Elm House, Ship Street. Mr Taylor was a huge man who rode around East Grinstead in a chaise, putting considerable strain on its springs. The shop closed in about 1929 and since 1971 has been Rentokil House.

C. & H. Gasson Ltd, timber and builders' merchants, at 153–7 London Road in the late 1920s. Standing in front of the premises are, left to right: Clement Gasson, who founded the business with his brother Henry in about 1894; Arthur Gasson, one of Clement's sons; Gilbert Wood, ultimately to become general manager and a director; and Percy Gasson, another of Clement's sons, who, along with his brother Horace, would later succeed to the business upon the death of their father in 1939. The firm closed in January 1980.

Circus elephants plod up London Road, 1904/5, watched by the spellbound townsfolk. Taken from Rock Gardens (now the Whitehall), this picture also shows E. Godley's sweetshop on the west side. (A. Harding)

Soldiers, including cyclists, on their way to France, 10 September 1914. The photographer, who with his two sisters ran a grocery on Lingfield Road, was a conscientious objector but nevertheless took a set of photographs of this eyecatching spectacle in London Road and no doubt sold many copies over the counter. (V.E. Morris)

The coronation of George V, celebrated in London Road by a procession, 22 June 1911. The local Church Lads Brigade is seen marching past Ellis & Palmer's premises, followed by the orphans from St Margaret's Convent. A stirring spectacle indeed! (A. Harding)

The opening of an entirely new Co-operative Stores at 115 London Road, a great occasion for the supporters of Socialism. It was performed by Isobel Macdonald, the eldest daughter of the Prime Minister in the Labour Government that was in power from 1929 to 1931. (H. Connold)

East Grinstead to Brighton walk. June. 16.07.

Not perhaps as spectacular as the *Tour de France*, but this assembly outside East Grinstead Post Office in London Road makes quite a show as it prepares to start for Brighton at 8.25 a.m., 16 June 1907. The shorts they are wearing are certainly no worse than those seen today. The boys sporting waistcoats and watchchains somehow succeed in their desire to look and feel 'grown up'.

Lined up outside 175 London Road, the East Grinstead Motor Garage Ltd (which was between Moat Church and the White Lion), these children in fancy dress are at the St James's Road area VE Day street party, May 1945. On the left, the 'clown' is Stuart Salter and the tall girl near him is his sister Maureen. A seven-year-old Michael Leppard (who was to become a distinguished schoolmaster and local historian) may be seen holding the shoulders of his sister Evelyn. The girl in the tall hat, near a pillar, is Nancy Friend, the daughter of a bus driver; she was to become a conductress on the local buses. (Harold Connold)

Top of Blackwell Hollow by the entrance to East Court, a private house, in the early 1900s. The entrance has since been altered in deference to Estcots Drive, built in about 1974. (W. Page)

Cantelupe Road looking south, with an unexpected tree in the middle! When the road was made in the 1890s the tree was allowed to remain, at least until the 1900s. The house behind is of interest too: the left-hand part, Tor Leven, was the residence of F.M. Wilcox, the High Street saddler; and in the 1920s W.H Davies, the poet and 'supertramp', lived there.

Bottom of Dunnings Road, looking north-east,' with West Hoathly Road behind the photographer. Unfortunately Dunnings Mill is out of shot on the left, but the horse and trap make a good focal point for the picture. ·

Green Hedges Avenue from London Road, showing the ivy-covered Urban District Council offices, a dog of indeterminate breed and, in the pre-motor age, the inevitable horse-droppings. The picture was sent as a Christmas card by the wife of W.E. Woollam, the UDC surveyor and sanitary inspector, to W.H. Hills, the journalist, in about 1905. (W. Page)

An exquisitely composed shot of the pretty Hermitage Lane, near the bottom (south) end, *c.* 1908. The Hermitage was a house so named by Thomas Wakeham, a solicitor, who lived there in the late eighteenth century; it was demolished in 1979. (P.E. Tombs)

Lewes Road, originally New Road, built in about 1826 to supersede Old Road, whose approach at the east end of the town was precipitous in the extreme. A cart has the road to itself on a glorious summer's day in about 1905. (W. Page)

Lingfield Road and Arthur Fry's butcher's shop on the corner of Dormans Park Road, looking south-east, *c.* 1912. Later its frontage was extended to the right. The shop was, and still is, famed for its homemade sausages. (V.E. Morris)

Lingfield Road looking south-east, opposite Highfield Road. These late nineteenth-century semi-detached houses are on the east side of Lingfield Road; some are dated 1882. Larger houses for the well-to-do were built on the west side of this road. (A. Harding)

Moat Road looks quite busy with two horse-drawn coal carts, of which one is owned by Hall & Co., 1905. This view looking north was taken near the London Road junction and also shows Moat Villas, which still exist. (W. Page)

Views of North End – that indeterminate area between East Grinstead and Felbridge – are very rare. To enliven the picture the photographer has positioned two children – possibly his own – and on the left of this north-facing view are Yaxley Cottages, dated 1878. (W. Page)

Grocery delivery in St James's Road by horse-drawn cart and a suspicious-looking delivery boy. One great advantage the horse had over the motor was that it could move along to the next house while its driver was delivering at the previous one. (A. Harding)

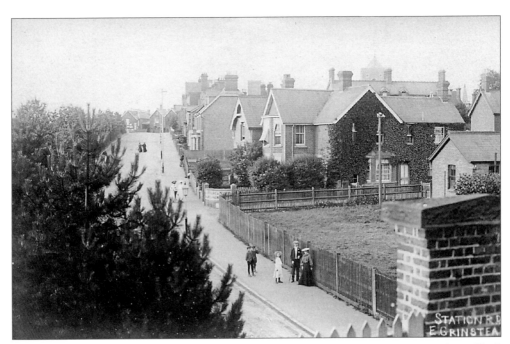

Station Road as seen from the now-vanished High Level railway station, built in 1882. The paddock belonged to Messrs Stone & Nutt, who set up as horse-cab proprietors and riding instructors in 1905. Next to that is Harold Nutt's house, now demolished. What would the two ladies walking in the middle of the road think of today's traffic? (W. Page)

EAST GRINSTEAD
BUILDINGS & OPEN SPACES

Moat Farm, which dated back to at least the eighteenth century and presumably was named after Moat Pond, c. 1902. Both the farm and the traditional haystacks have long since vanished. (W. Page)

Blackwell Farm and its house, seen from the bottom of Blackwell Hollow, 1928. Its earliest known reference is dated 1594. It was demolished some years after this photograph was taken and the land purchased for making the Blackwell Farm Estate in 1952. (H. Connold)

Estcots Farmhouse, north elevation. It is a mainly fifteenth-century hall house with seventeenth-century additions on the north side and a nineteenth-century addition on the west side. At one stage it was altered to form two cottages, but was later restored to one. (A. Harding)

Pictures of East Grinstead Vicarage taken before it was seriously damaged by fire on 27 February 1908 are quite rare. This is the western aspect in about 1880, as it looked after alterations made in 1848. (H.T. Melville)

The National Schools, later renamed successively the Board, Council and Chequer Mead schools, were opened in 1861 and closed in 1990. Designed by Parsons of Lewes, they were built by Robert Pink of East Grinstead. Also seen here is the Playfield being used for its proper purpose, in about 1900. (W. Page)

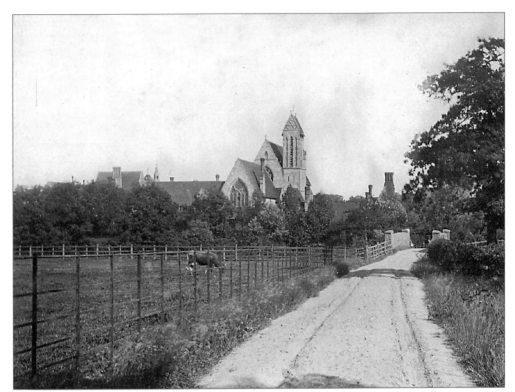

Durkins Farm, view looking south-east, *c.* 1905. Only St Margaret's Convent chapel and the railway bridge give meaning to the picture, the foreground of which is now obliterated by Charlwoods Road and light industrial buildings. (W. Page)

A closer view of St Margaret's Convent, looking west from its garden. The chapel of 1883, by G.E. Street, is the left-hand part. (W. Page)

St Margaret's Convent quadrangle, looking north-west, 1909. The sisters moved into new premises nearby in 1975 and the old Convent was later adapted into apartments. (F. Frith & Co.)

Blockfield, believed to be fourteenth century and owned for generations by the Gainsford family. In 1922 architect George Crawley added north and south wings and it was renamed Old Surrey Hall. It lies off Holtye Road about 2 miles east of the town. Henry VIII is said to have stayed there while wooing Anne Boleyn; and during restoration work in the 1920s ghostly footsteps were heard!

Hipsfield, off Old Road, still looking very new and stark. It was built in 1912 and its first owner was the Revd Charles H. Price, minister of Zion Chapel from 1909 to 1914. In the left background are glimpsed houses in College Lane. (A. Harding)

This open space, seen from the north-east in about 1905, is now Brooklands Park. The hedge near the skyline on the right marks where Brooklands Way would be laid out, and the cottages just visible still stand at the bottom of West Hill. (W. Page)

Queen's Road cemetery, c. 1904. It was opened in February 1869. This view shows the east elevation of the chapels (designed by Parsons of Lewes and built in 1869 by Robert Pink of East Grinstead) and, bottom left, the gravestone of Thomas Cramp, the town's most famous total abstainer, who died in August 1891. Today the chapels are private dwellings. (A. Harding)

A rather brave young lady greets a pair of swans and their cygnets on Moat Pond, *c.* 1905. The pond, which never was a moat but was so named probably because of its moat-like shape, is nowadays considered too small to support swans. (W. Page)

Moat Pond, looking south-east from Moat Road, in June 1947. This picture first appeared in the 1948 edition of *East Grinstead – The Official Guide* with the two children on the right painted out; one wonders why. (H. Connold)

Imberhorne Park, *c.* 1902. This was the extensive ground of Sir Edward Blount's residence, Imberhorne, and presumably had been opened to the public for the day, with W. & J. Evershed, fruiterers of Lingfield Road, having set up a stall to cater for the visitors. Those standing behind the stall, left to right, are: Bert Everest, Mrs Evershed, -?- , Mr Evershed, Cyril Stairs, Mr Wood and Mr Smith. (A. Harding)

Saint Hill Green, with the road to Hazelden and Felbridge on the left and that to East Grinstead (1½ miles) via Dunnings on the right, *c.* 1905. The three boys look like early models for William Brown and the Outlaws.

Saint Hill House, 1¼ miles south-west of East Grinstead, *c.* 1906. Between 1728 and 1883 it was owned by members of the Crawfurd family but when this picture was taken its owner was Edgar March Crookshank, who in the 1906 General Election had the unhappy distinction of being the only Unionist candidate for East Grinstead ever to be defeated by a Liberal.

EAST GRINSTEAD PEOPLE

Colonel Ralph Stephenson Clarke, East Grinstead's Conservative Member of Parliament from July 1936 to May 1955. Born in August 1892, he served in the Sussex Yeomanry in 1914, becoming a Lieutenant-Colonel, Royal Artillery, in 1939. He was a director of the coal merchants Stephenson Clarke, whose railway wagons were once a common sight in the south of England. A typical country gentleman, his hobbies were horticulture, hunting and fishing. He died in May 1970.

Harold Connold, Member of the Institute of British Photographers, shortly before his retirement in 1959. Born in May 1889, he was East Grinstead's best-known professional photographer, first at 23 High Street from 1926 and then at No. 15 between about 1931 and June 1959. A Rotarian and Urban District councillor from the late 1930s, he was elected chairman of the UDC in 1949. He was a pioneer of home movie-making with colour film in 1939. He died in May 1968. (Edna Connold)

Arthur Perry, c. 1940. He came to East Grinstead from Aylesbury in 1939 and acquired the drapery business of Young & Sons at 43–9 High Street. Elected to the Urban District Council in March 1942, he became Chairman in 1945 and again in 1950, being the first to wear the now familiar chain of office. A Rotarian, and for ten years secretary of Moat Congregational Church, he was a very dignified gentleman who devoted his life to the service of others. He died in March 1957. (Harold Connold)

Brian Desmond, chief reporter of the *East Grinstead Observer*, at work in his office at 64 London Road in the 1950s. This triple exposure was made, unknown to the subject, by one of the paper's own photographers. Brian Desmond joined the *Observer* in 1921 and within a few years was covering all the main East Grinstead news stories. In the 1950s he also wrote leaders, articles of general interest as 'Townsman', church notes as 'Layman', sporting notes as 'Touch Judge' and children's short stories. He founded East Grinstead Rugby Football Club in 1929 and was its secretary for thirty-four years. He retired from journalism in 1967 and died in December 1995 aged ninety-two.

Sarah Norman Neale, the wife of Dr John Mason Neale, with one of their daughters (probably Sarah Agnes, the eldest) at Sackville College, East Grinstead, *c.* 1855. Dr Neale was warden of Sackville College – an almshouse founded in 1608 – from 1846 to 1866. This very early photograph is believed to have been taken by the nationally famous Joseph Cundall (1818–95).

Presentation to George Herbert Pattern (left) at the Clarendon Restaurant, East Grinstead, 12 March 1965, to mark his retirement as organist and choirmaster at St Swithun's Church. Making the presentation is Alan Huggett (Parochial Church Council); seated are Mrs Lewis Bennett and the Revd Canon Harry Copsey, vicar of East Grinstead.

Charles Chevall Tooke, JP, of Hurst-an-Clays, seated on 'Bramshaw' in the 1880s. The third son of Thomas Tooke, economist and free-trader, Charles was one of the directors of the East Grinstead Railway Co. in the 1850s. In 1860 he gave land to divert Ship Street so that it no longer passed his frontage. Soon after his death in October 1890 his large and ugly pew in the parish church was removed!

Joseph Rice (1855–1935), director of the engineering firm of Rice Bros, incorporated in 1893. As chairman of East Grinstead Urban District Council in 1905, 1909 and 1912 he doubtless held himself in high regard, and this portrait was sent by him to W.H. Hills, the town's leading journalist, as a Christmas card in 1905.

Richard L. Treble (1879–1941), the first headmaster of East Grinstead County (Grammar) School from 1928 to 1938. He abolished homework in 1931. A colleague, Philip Sandall, wrote in 1941: 'His study door was always open . . . his work was put aside when his advice was sought.' This portrait was made in July 1938. (Harold Connold)

George 'Juggy' Wren, a porter-signalman at East Grinstead railway station, proudly shows off his granddaughter outside Harold Nutt's house in Station Road, c. 1922. 'Juggy' was a Sussex name for 'wren'. The perambulator is thought to be a 'Dunkley' which would have been quite expensive. (Kenneth Nutt)

The East Grinstead Military and Town Prize Band poses in the vicarage garden, *c.* 1910. Frank Brinkhurst, the undertaker (who died in September 1926), is seen with a double bass. To his right is the Revd Wilfrid Wadham Youard, vicar of East Grinstead from November 1908 to May 1924 and later Dean of Battle. (Arthur Harding)

A Caledonian Dance, complete with kilts and bagpipes, at the Queen's Hall, East Grinstead, 19 February 1913. One wonders if there were many genuine Scots among the assembly. (East Grinstead Photo Co.)

At the Civic Arts Hall in West Street, Miss Janet Sargent, director of the local bus company Sargents of East Grinstead, shows her model bus to the over sixties, November 1951. It appears to be based on the Bedford 'OB', of which the company had four examples. Third from left is Mrs Brooker (who lived to be 100) and fourth is Mrs Westgate. (*East Grinstead Observer*)

East Grinstead Bowling Club, 1913. The location is the West Street cricket ground, which in winter was used by the football club. In this group there is a higher proportion of ladies than in most other sporting groups of the time. (A. Harding)

East Grinstead Football Club team, 1930. Back row, left to right: -?-, Arthur Mills, Lionel Spearman, -?-, -?-. Middle row: Tommy Hall, Stan Furminger, Les Charlwood, -?-, Tim Rowe. Front row: Harry Carter, Stan Draper, Harry Stratton, Stan Carter, Algy Shepherd.

Nutt Brothers' stableyard, Station Road, East Grinstead, *c.* 1911. Driving the landau (left) is Albert Buddle, with Tom Hayward standing behind it. The little lad on the pony is Kenneth Nutt, son of the proprietor Harold Nutt, who is seen on horseback next to him. In the centre is a carriage and pair, and riding side-saddle is Mrs Nutt. On the extreme left may be glimpsed Jack Pentecost, who is shaking a sieve of corn to make the horses' ears prick up, no doubt at the request of the photographer. (Edgar Kinsey)

One of Hall & Co.'s East Grinstead delivery carts with a magnificent shire horse, *c.* 1935. The likelihood is that this assembly had been specially prepared for a May Day horse parade. (Harold Connold)

ASHURST WOOD &
HAMMERWOOD

Avery's Post Office and Stores in the 1930s. This shop, which still exists, was opened in 1907 and Kate Avery was grocer and sub-postmistress until her death in 1940. The Maypole Inn, opened in 1879, was owned by the Southdown & East Grinstead Breweries until March 1924, when Tamplins purchased it.

View looking west from Woods Hill Lane, possibly early 1920s. The roof of the original St Dunstan's Church is seen near the large tree on the left of the picture. The sender of this card in 1941 remarked that the 'place is very altered too many houses now'. (H.H. Camburn)

Top of Wall Hill, Ashurst Wood, looking north. This road was originally part of the London–Lewes turnpike until the 'Brambletye Bends' diversion was made in 1826. In the centre is the forge, dating from the early 1900s. (H.H. Camburn)

Dirty Lane (in Ashurst Wood) is not a description of its condition but its actual name. It leads off from School Lane and, although no longer grass-grown as shown here, is still little more than a track.

Yewhurst Lodge, looking east from Hammerwood Road, Ashurst Wood. Yewhurst itself (now The Abbey) was the home of Sir Abe Bailey (1864–1940), a South African. Since this early twentieth-century view was recorded the ivy and tree in the centre have disappeared and the building is called the Gate Lodge. (Avery's Photo Series)

The original St Dunstan's Church, opened in 1884, on the Lewes Road. The boy selling flowers is Arthur 'Rip' Cooper, born 1911, and so the picture can be dated to about 1920. The church was closed in 1979 and is now a private house.

Ashurst Wood School group, c. 1900. The headmaster is William Clayton Bennett, who held that position from 1895 to 1914. After receiving a presentation on 26 February 1914, he wrote in the school log book: 'It is some little compensation for over 18 years work to know that one's work is appreciated by some.'

An ox being roasted at The Beeches, Ashurst Wood. Local worthy Mrs Simpson is doing the carving. This coronation celebration went ahead as scheduled, on 26 June 1902, even though the actual coronation had been postponed to 9 August 1902 owing to Edward VII's illness. (Carr & Hopperton, East Grinstead)

Nenthorn House, after a fire, possibly 1900s. It was so named by the Congregational Minister, the Revd Benjamin Slight, after Nenthorn, Berwickshire, where he had lived. He died on 17 August 1889. The house was repaired and still stands next to the former Congregational Church (now Anglican).

Thornhill, about ¾ mile east of Ashurst Wood. Built in 1790, it was part of the Hammerwood Estate, possibly the bailiff's house, and by 1812 was being described as a manor farm.

The Homestall, before its reconstruction, *c.* 1900. Built in about 1300, it was enlarged after 1900 by Lord Dewar, the whisky magnate, and in 1932–5 was enlarged again by his nephew, John Dewar, using the fabric of Dutton Hall, Cheshire (built 1539–42), transported south in sixty lorry loads. The house was then renamed Dutton Homestall. (H. Connold)

Dutton Homestall Convalescent Hospital, 1940. The house was adapted as a convalescent hospital for officers on 2 March 1940. John Dewar, its owner, died in 1954 and since 1965 the place has been Stoke Brunswick School. (H. Connold)

At Homestall Kennels (now riding stables). Arthur 'Rip' Cooper (centre) holds a greyhound while John Dewar, seated, watches. From 1932 'Rip' Cooper was Mr Dewar's driver, taking greyhounds all over the country. This picture dates from the mid to late 1930s.

Homestall Poultry Farm, Ashurst Wood. During the late 1920s/early 1930s Walter Bradley, poultry farm manager to Lord Dewar of Homestall, lived here. The house, which no longer exists, is believed to have stood west of Shovelstrode, a mile north of the village. (H.H. Camburn)

Ashurst Wood Junior Cricket Team, *c.* 1960. In the back row are (fourth from left) Graham Power and (sixth from left) ? West. The man is John Rose, founder of the junior cricket club.

The Three Crowns, Ashurst Wood, with the coaches more prominent than the pub, *c.* 1931. Left is Timpson's AEC Reliance No. 176; centre: Birch Bros Leyland Lioness No. K18; right: a Leyland Cub of Blue Belle. The Three Crowns has been traced to 1725, though the present frontage appears to be a reconstruction dating from the 1900s. (RAP Co. Ltd)

Hammerwood, one of only two houses in England designed by Benjamin Latrobe (1764–1820), dates from 1792. John Dorrien Magens, chairman of the East Grinstead Railway Co. in the 1850s, owned this house from 1848. In August 1982 it was purchased by David Pinnegar just in time to prevent its collapse after years of neglect and was restored by him. (W. Page)

A beautiful spring day at Hammerwood School with lessons being taken outside, 1906. Arthur Harding and his camera were on hand to record a scene probably taken for granted then. The school, built by local benefactor Oswald Smith in 1873, closed in 1959. (A. Harding)

FOREST ROW, HARTFIELD & COLEMAN'S HATCH

The garage (Hunnisett & King), c. 1914. The motor cars, from left to right, are a Renault, a Spyher and a Flanders. The motor cycle is a 7 h.p. Chater Lea from about 1913.

Forest Row, The Square, looking north, *c.* 1904. Stephen Jones, the baker, was in business until his death in November 1924. On the left is a gas lamp belonging to the Brambletye Hotel. (Photochrom Co. Ltd)

The Square showing the post office, two early motor cars, Jones the baker and Martin's the drapers, *c.* 1912. When Stephen Jones died his two daughters carried on with the bakery; after 1945 Mr Wood took it over. (Sayers Bros)

Forest Row looking south, after the relaying of the green, *c.* 1938. The village hall (left of centre) was built in 1892; its architect was J.M. Brydon and Job Luxford of Forest Row was the builder. In the centre of this picture is Holy Trinity Church (1836) and on the right, Martin's Garage. (Raphael Tuck & Sons

Forest Row looking north, showing the village hall, 1948. On the left is one of the many road signs provided by the Royal Automobile Club to the same standard as the official Ministry of Transport items. High up, overlooking the village, is the Abbey School, previously Ashurst Wood Abbey, formerly Yewhurst. (Photochrom Co. Ltd)

Forest Row railway station, looking north-east from Station Road, possibly in the 1880s as everything still looks pristine. The station, which was opened on 1 October 1866, was most inconveniently sited at the end of this long road, which was constructed and maintained by the railway company. The railway closed on 1 January 1967.

This view of Station Road shows its great length, the station just visible at the end. On the left is the Railway Hotel, which was renamed the Foresters Arms after the railway closed. In recent times it has lost its porch. (Sayers Bros)

Forest Row Holy Trinity Church in the 1950s. Its architect was William Moseley and it was built in 1836 in the Gothic style, its spire being at the north end. The side aisle was added in 1877–9 by Herbert Green. (H. Connold)

The Brambletye Hotel, *c.* 1904. The section on the right, obscured by a tree, is now known as Black Peter's Bar. According to A. Conan Doyle, Sherlock Holmes, investigating the death of 'Black Peter' Carey, arrived in Forest Row in July 1895 and stayed at the hotel for the night. (Photochrom Co. Ltd)

The window display of Bernard and George Martin, drapers, in the Square, Forest Row in the 1900s. The exterior illumination is by gas.

J.C. Finch, the muffin man, stands in the Square on a damp day with his wares and bell in the 1920s. He lived in Lingfield and regularly walked to Forest Row, calling in at hostelries on the way. His crumpets were made by Curtis's bakery in East Grinstead. B. & G. Martin's shop is seen across the street.

Forest Row, Chapel Lane, looking south-east, in the early 1900s. Park Cottages, on the left, are dated 1880. On the right is the yard of the Bethesda Baptist Chapel. (Sayers Bros)

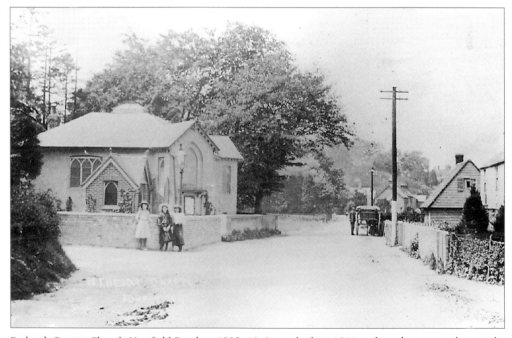

Bethesda Baptist Chapel, Hartfield Road, *c*. 1905–10. It was built in 1811, enlarged two years later at the western end and rebuilt into its present form before 1914. The minister from 1846 to 1853, the Revd George Veals, was struck by lightning in August 1852 but recovered; he died in 1879.

Tablehurst, just east of Forest Row railway station, *c.* 1900. It is timber-framed, tile-hung and roofed in Horsham stone on the west side. In 1754 one John Major owned the house, but by 1933 the farmhouse had been modernized and belonged to Lord Ellenborough. (W. Page, East Grinstead)

Tablehurst water mill, *c.* 1905. This stood near the miller's house but was burnt down in the 1930s. (Sayers Bros)

Forest Row Church of England School girls – and one boy, *c.* 1900. Back row, fourth from left: Nellie Parker. Next row, standing, second from right: Frances Bishop. Third row, seated, second from left: Hetty Weeding; fourth: Edith Parker; sixth: Edith Bishop. Front row, first from right: Ernest Bishop. who was in the infants class. There is a good variety of expressions in this group.

An outing from Forest Row to the British Empire Exhibition at Wembley in 1924 by a charabanc provided by Autocar of Tunbridge Wells. The four boys in the foreground are (left to right) John Jackson (uniquely hatless), the Russells and Bob Smithers jnr. Mrs Smithers is to his left and Bob Smithers snr is to the left of the group of four men by the vehicle.

Abe Mitchell, the world-renowned golfer. Born in 1887 on Ashdown Forest, close to the Royal Ashdown Forest Golf Club, he won his first golf trophy as an amateur in 1910 and turned professional three years later. In the 1920s he won many cups in both Britain and the USA, and he was a member of the Artisan section of the Royal Ashdown Forest Golf Club. His career lasted thirty-three years until the Second World War and he died aged sixty in 1948. F. Pignon wrote that he was 'one of golf's greatest gentlemen'.

Gwen Lally in July 1929, during the Pageant of Ashdown Forest, of which she was the producer, at Kidbrooke Park, Forest Row. This open-air pageant, with performances portraying various historical periods, raised money for a new wing to the village hall and for five county hospitals.

Empire Day, Forest Row School, 24 May 1927. The children are in costumes of various countries representing the then British Empire. Back row, from left: seventh, Reg Eames; eighth, Mr Stringer (head teacher, boys); ninth, Dann; tenth, Alf Richardson; twelfth, Joe Smith. Middle row, from left: eighth, Ella Blackstone; ninth, Edwards; tenth, Minnie Crowhurst; eleventh, Mrs Stringer (head teacher, girls). Front row, from left: Ina Blackstone, Bertha Southey, Grace Card, Esme Woodrow, Percy Elderfield and seventh from the left, Sybil Woodrow. The unidentified 'Rajah' in the front should have won first prize if any were being offered.

Pageant of Ashdown Forest, July 1929. Some of the committee and celebrities are seen here at Kidbrooke Park; the Duchess of York (later Queen Elizabeth) was a patron. Back row, from left: Lord Edward Gleichen (chairman), Olaf Hambro (owner of Kidbrooke Park), Rudyard Kipling, Gwen Lally (producer), Sir Stanley Colville. Front row: Lady Gleichen, Winifred Hambro, the Duchess of York, her sister, Mrs Kipling, Lady Colville.

A scene from the Pageant of Ashdown Forest, in Kidbrooke Park, July 1929. Left to right: Eric Martin, Grace Blackstone, Pat Wheller, Ethel King, Sybil Martin. (Harold G. Bailey, Godalming)

Canadians in a 'Wings for Victory' parade drive through Forest Row during the Second World War, possibly in 1942. General Coffin takes the salute outside the village hall. The village is unlikely to witness such a spectacle again. Compare the frontage of Hunnisett's garage with that shown in the picture on page 61.

A carefully posed shot of Harman's meat float, decorated for a carnival, *c.* 1921. Its driver is Sid Ford. The horse is becoming impatient with the delay, pawing the ground and nodding his head. The footpath seen in the centre background leads to Spring Meadow.

Forest Row Band, *c.* 1950. Formed by 1895, it was disbanded in August 1936, reformed in 1937 and finally ceased in the early 1950s. Here the bandmaster is Arthur Francis; back row, extreme right, Harry Terry; in the middle row from left: Marion Barlow, Albert Raffan, Mary and Joan Maclean, Sheila Saunders and John Crowhurst. The boys in the front are Stuart and Geoffrey Ridley.

Brambletye 'Castle' ruins, near Forest Row, looking north-east in the early 1900s. Dated 1631, the structure was begun by Sir Henry Compton but by the nineteenth century it was partly decayed and partly demolished. The ivy was removed in about 1930. (Photochrom Co. Ltd)

Bolebroke Castle gatehouse, 1¼ miles north of Hartfield. It was built between 1475 and 1500 in red brick; note the similarity of the tower pinnacles to the one surviving at Brambletye 'Castle', above. The manor of Bolebroke was owned by Earl de la Warr. (F. Medhurst)

Hartfield High Street, looking north, *c.* 1914. A little girl is entranced by the window display of F. Jacques, the baker. Today, this shop sells souvenirs of Winnie the Pooh, whose adventures took place not far from here. (H. Camburn)

Hartfield High Street, looking south-west, 1928. The public house, now known as the Hay Waggon, was then called the Dorset Arms, offering luncheons, teas and dinners. On the extreme right is Vine House Cottage, next to it the tiny Post Office Stores, then Primrose Cottage with its weatherboarding. (H. Connold)

Charity dole at Hartfield Church, by the tomb of Nicholas Smith. Will Groombridge is receiving his share from the rector (the Revd Mr James) and churchwarden (Ernest Divall) on a Good Friday in the late 1930s. Smith had left an annual charge of £5 on Cotchford Farm, the owner of which had to pay this sum to the Church every year. Cotchford Farm was the home of the writer Alan Alexander Milne from 1924 to 1956.

The Gallipot Inn, half a mile south-west of Hartfield, *c.* 1898. The licensee was William W. Sands, who also sold tobacco. The inn is little changed externally – the right-hand doorway has been given a porch and the wooden fence has been removed.

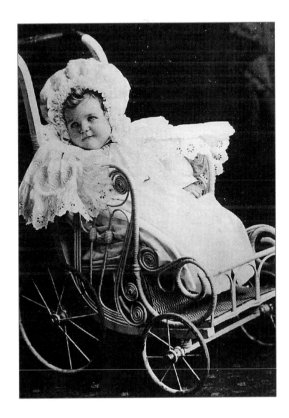

Letitia Smith, the granddaughter of William Sands, 1909.

Brackenhill Open-air School, *c.* 1928. This establishment, owned by Mrs K. Harvey, was off the Hartfield road, between the Gallipot and Coleman's Hatch church, and the school house was demolished only a few years ago. All lessons were taken in the open and covered accommodation was extremely basic. The school closed in 1939.

Agriculture as practised in bygone times with Suffolk Punches. At North Clays (about 1½ miles north-west of Hartfield by footpath) Harry Humphrey, with Clansman and Amanda, does the harvesting, not later than 1947. The horses often appeared at ploughing matches and were well known in Sussex.

Coleman's Hatch church, May 1951. It was designed by the architects A. Blomfield & Sons. There was no real need for a new church so close to Hartfield's, and Coleman's Hatch was not a populous district; but nevertheless several parishioners dissatisfied with the then rector of Hartfield subscribed to its construction in 1912/13. (H. Connold)

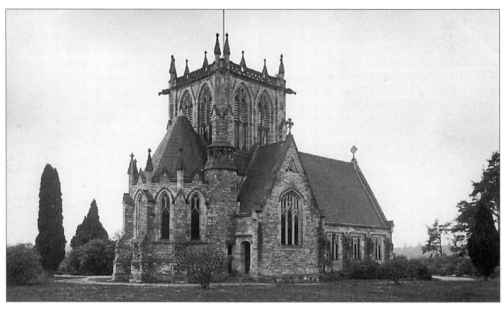

St Richard de Wych Church, Ashdown Park, near Coleman's Hatch, possibly early 1920s. Built in 1886/7 it was reputedly based on St Mary's, Beverley, Yorkshire. Abe Mitchell, the famous golfer, was christened there. Closed in 1940, it was demolished during 1974/5. (H. Camburn)

The Hatch Inn, Coleman's Hatch, looking south. Both the inn and the sandstone house (right) are little changed externally today. Could Coleman's Hatch have been the inspiration for 'Woodman's Lee', the fictitious village in the Sherlock Holmes story 'Black Peter' (see page 65). (H. Connold)

A Sussex farmstead, near Coleman's Hatch, May 1939. Its exact location has not been established; perhaps it no longer exists. Oast houses, although more associated with Kent, are occasionally found in Sussex, especially in those parts near the Kent boundary. (H. Connold)

Chuck Hatch, a hamlet 2 miles south of Hartfield. A splendidly varied group gathers outside the store, with bicycles and a horse and trap to add interest, in about 1900. The lady wearing a white lace cap is Mrs Elliott, the shop's owner; her daughter – who actually ran the shop – is seen to the right in a white blouse. The business closed in about 1918 but the building itself survives, although much altered. Incidentally, a 'hatch' was an ancient gate of Ashdown Forest.

DORMANSLAND, LINGFIELD & FELBRIDGE

Dormansland, The Platt ('open land'), an idyllic scene of the 1900s showing H. Stone's General Stores nestling almost hidden in the trees. Three brands of tea are advertised outside — Home & Colonial, Liptons and Mazzawattee.

Dormansland, Parish Church of St John, 1909. The church opened on 14 April 1882 and the architect was Arthur Blomfield. In 1909 the lychgate had just been added and in 1914 the church itself was enlarged by the addition of a south aisle. (Kingsway Series)

Dormansland High Street, looking north, c. 1910. On the right is the Royal Oak, an early nineteenth-century house; two huge bushes frame its doorway.

The Plough Inn, looking south-east, *c.* 1910. This timber-framed house was built in about 1500 and incorporates eighteenth- and nineteenth-century additions. There have been few changes since this photograph was taken but the shed on the left is gone. On the extreme right is Dormans Cottage. (Stripp's Series)

Dormansland Forge in the 1930s or '40s. On the right is the proprietor Frank Skinner, who lived in the adjoining house. The other man is his assistant, Gordon Mayo, who came to the village aged eighteen to work under Frank Skinner's father. Some of the tools and artefacts from this forge may be seen at East Grinstead Town Museum.

Open-top bus No. 210 (AEC/Short, 1928) of East Surrey Traction Co. at Dormansland Plough, 1928. The driver is John Lawson and the conductor is Leonard Odell, who later became a Green Line coach driver. Route 404 ran between Oxted and East Grinstead via Edenbridge from October 1926 to April 1930.

Dormans railway station, *c.* 1905. Outside stands the stationmaster in gold braid. This station, opened on 10 March 1884, has always been very rural and remote from most habitations; it is a good mile from the village centre. (A.G. Wheller)

The beautiful Cooks Pond, Dormans Park, and the viaduct that spans it, *c.* 1908. This fine structure, which was opened on 10 March 1884, is about 650 ft long and 65 ft high, with five spans. To allow for its construction the pond needed to be drained, but by 1890 it had refilled. (P.E. Tombs)

Dormans Park Hotel, *c.* 1900. The hotel opened in 1893, but had started life five years earlier as the clubhouse for the Bellaggio Estate Ltd, which soon failed. By 1900 the hotel was owned by William Christopher (of the catering firm Letheby & Christopher). Closure came about in 1952 and demolition in the early 1960s. (Valentine)

Dormans Park is a very exclusive residential area between East Grinstead and Dormansland. In 1909 it was served by the exotic Bungalow Post Office – 'Woodside' – which stood a short distance west of the railway bridge. After closure in January 1933 it became a private residence but was later demolished. (F. Frith & Co.)

Lingfield Old Town, 1909. On the left is Faulkner's butcher's shop, Pollard House, a mid-fifteenth-century Wealden building. The other buildings are mainly seventeenth century, and the Church of St Peter and St Paul is in the background. George Faulkner died in 1911 and the shop was years later converted into a private residence. (Kingsway Series)

Lingfield, Church Road, in the 1920s. Apparently the gentlemen have just come off an afternoon train from London. The Star Hotel on the corner of Old Town is now Church House. (Taylors, Eastbourne)

Lingfield, the guest house, viewed from the churchyard in 1909. Of late fifteenth-century origin, and said to have been the guest house of Lingfield College, it was restored in 1896 by its then owner, Forster Hayward, FSA. It is now a public library. (Kingsway Series)

The Old Cage, Lingfield, *c.* 1910. Although a gentleman is posing rather self-consciously inside it, this is some years after the last petty offender was incarcerated there (1882). In the 1950s and '60s the only occupant was an 'ordinary' bicycle (a penny-farthing). (J. Jupp)

The Gun Pit Pond with The Cage and the base of St Peter's Cross (fifteenth century) behind it, spring 1954. The cross itself has long disappeared. The sandstone lock-up known as The Cage was built in 1773. (E.A. Sweetman & Son Ltd)

Lingfield Council School, showing a girls' physical fitness class, c. 1936. The school opened in June 1907. On the left, the corrugated iron structure – the 'tinner' – housed cookery and woodwork classrooms until 1937/8, when it was replaced by a two-storey wing to the west of the main building. (Doris Jenner)

An 'RF' bus on route 428, Dormansland to East Grinstead, at Lingfield post office, 23 February 1970. The operator is London Country Bus Services but the vehicle, in red livery, is on hire from London Transport. (D. Gould)

Another bus on route 428 picks up schoolgirls in Lingfield High Street at 4.10 p.m., 23 February 1970. This journey was the only one worked by Crawley garage; the Merlin Standee bus was an unpopular and short-lived type. In the right background may be seen the secondary school with the two-storey wing mentioned earlier. (D. Gould)

Felbridge, the Parish Church of St John the Divine, looking south-east, *c.* 1910. Its architect was William White and it was completed in 1865 using local stone. It was paid for by George Gatty, of Felbridge Place. (East Grinstead Photo Co.)

Looking north to the eighteenth-century Star Inn at Felbridge, 1925. It has changed little since then apart from a daub of pink paint on its wall tiles. A 'K'-type open-top bus running from Uckfield to West Croydon (route S9) pauses on its leisurely journey. (F. Frith & Co.)

Charles Henry Gatty, LLD (1836–1903), aged about thirty. He was the son of George Gatty of Felbridge Place, which Charles inherited in 1864. Dr Gatty, who was a JP for Surrey and Sussex, had the right to appoint the vicar ('advowson') of Felbridge Church and until May 1887 he was president of East Grinstead Town Band. After the band had played at a celebration of which he disapproved, he resigned and withdrew his support, although by the mid-1890s he had resumed his patronage of the band again. He died on 12 December 1903, aged sixty-seven.

Felbridge Place, built in the eighteenth century and reconstructed in the nineteenth century. It was the home of James Evelyn, and George Gatty purchased it in 1855. In the 1930s and '40s it was the Felbridge Place Hotel, as seen here, a country house with large rooms, surrounded by old trees and extensive grounds. Its site is now occupied by Whittington College.

The 'Evelyn Chestnuts' on Crawley Down Road, Felbridge, looking east in the 1930s. They were planted in the seventeenth century, and were certainly well established by 1745. (H. Connold)

The Evelyn Monument, erected by James Evelyn (1718–93) of Felbridge Place in 1786 in memory of his father Edward. This sandstone column, 85-ft high, was designed by Sir John Soane and was located in the grounds of Felbridge Place, practically opposite the school. At its base was a carving of a snake biting its tail, representing Eternity. The monument was taken down in 1927/8 and removed to Lemmington Hall, Alnwick, Northumberland by Stephen Aitchison. (W. Harding)

Hedgecourt Lake and Mill Lane looking south-east, *c.* 1905. The former corn mill is now called Mill House and many trees have grown here since. The gentleman is doing his best to look casual, but is clearly aware of the photographer – perhaps a relative? (A. Harding)

Ward's Farm Lodge, 1911. Now called Ebor Lodge, it stands off the main London–Eastbourne road, half a mile north of the bridge at Felbridge. It housed the farm bailiff.

The funeral at Felbridge churchyard of a local policeman, 1898. PC James Baldwin was stabbed while on duty in London and died of his wounds on 2 October 1898 aged only twenty-nine. Several of his colleagues were among the mourners. (Smith & Co., Redhill)

A view showing the severe damage caused to Felbridge Vicarage by an air attack on 28 August 1940. The church also suffered some damage to its east and south sides. In 1965 the original vicarage, then 100 years old, was replaced by a new one on a different site.

Wire Mill, near Felbridge, looking west, *c.* 1899. Now the Wiremill Inn, the building has steps leading up to the doorway on the north-east wall. Woodcock Hammer was the original name of the wire mill, which it is said made nails used in the building of St Paul's Cathedral. (David Kennedy)

WORTH PARISH
(INCLUDING COPTHORNE, CRAWLEY DOWN & TURNERS HILL)

Burleigh House, Crawley Down, in the 1920s. This Wealden hall house was built in about 1400 and was later one of several places where Henry VIII is said to have courted Anne Boleyn. The house was demolished in 1936.

A scarcely recognizable view of the Parish Church of St Nicholas, Worth, *c.* 1869. It is a Saxon church dating fron the tenth century. Some years after this photograph was taken, the cement rendering was removed to reveal the beautiful stonework, the large window in the apse (right) was filled in, and the wooden spire was replaced with a stone one in 1871. The timber boards in the graveyard showing inscriptions soon decayed and new graves were marked out by stone slabs.

St Nicholas, Worth, south-east elevation, *c.* 1958. The two gravestones in the foreground, inscribed to Lucy Amy Briggs and Lilian Isabel Irons, date from 1956. In September 1986 the nineteenth-century nave roof was destroyed by fire but a new roof was built and the church reopened two years later. (H. Connold)

The Duke's Head, Copthorne, established by 1782, seen here extended in the early twentieth century. The left-hand part has been retained, much altered, but the right-hand portion was totally replaced with a two-gabled extension to match those on the left.

St John's Church, Copthorne, east elevation, c. 1925. The 'gothic' gravestone is inscribed to Charles Joseph Martin, who died in January 1922. (H.H. Camburn)

An aerial view of Copthorne Preparatory School, looking west, in the 1950s. Effingham Lane runs across the picture in the foreground. The school was formerly known as Emsworth House. (H. Connold)

A closer look at Copthorne Preparatory School buildings, west elevation, showing the tennis courts and the tower of the school chapel. The school, run by the Copthorne School Trust Ltd, is attended by four- to thirteen-year-olds. (H. Connold)

Crawley Down post office, Turners Hill Road, looking north, *c.* 1900. On the tricycle is Mr Smith, the postmaster. The houses in this picture, externally unchanged, stand near the junction with Sandy Lane.

Crawley Down, Bowers Place, showing a small newsagent's shop (now Elm House). The placards that read 'Prayer Book's Fate' and 'Fate of New Prayer Book' refer to the rejection by Parliament of the revised Book of Common Prayer in 1928. This picture must therefore date from that time.

Grange Road station level crossing, Crawley Down, *c.* 1905. The Royal Oak public house (1866) is on the far side of the railway line, but the station itself is obscured by trees on the left. The railway closed on 1 January 1967, but the Royal Oak survives, although its once beautiful brickwork has been painted over in recent times.

Crawley Down, Grange Road brickworks, showing a 'clamp', *c.* 1900. In the centre foreground is Albert Philpott, the foreman. The brickfield, one of four in the village, was south-east of Grange Road station, and the works ceased functioning in 1939.

Crawley Down Church of England Schools, looking north, *c*. 1905. Built in 1851, on the Turners Hill road, they were closed in 1982 and the buildings later incorporated into a housing scheme, 'Scholars Court'. The school house is hidden behind the main building.

Harris's grocery and drapery stores, at Snow Hill, Crawley Down, looking north-east, *c*. 1900. Since then there have been minor structural alterations, the tree has gone and the road has been widened. The shop is now The Bargain Boutique.

The Green, Turner's Hill, Sussex.

Turners Hill, a small village built on an eminence 558 ft above sea level, *c.* 1914. Sixteen children, including an errand boy with a wicker basket, pose for the photographer. The tree was removed in 1987, but a new one now grows in its place. (A.H. Homewood, Burgess Hill)

TURNERS HILL. SUSSEX.

Turners Hill, looking west from East Street towards Church Road, *c.* 1950. Forge House (The Bank) and Forge Cottage are in the centre, with the old forge – adapted for use as the village's fire station – to its left. The earliest reference to The Bank is 1802.(H. Connold)

Turners Hill, The Square and North Street, looking north, *c.* 1930. On the extreme left is Providence Terrace, dated 1901; in the centre, Castle's Stores, now Central Stores and Bakery; on the extreme right, Sunnyside, dated 1897. In 1972 Sunnyside received a twin-gabled southerly extension.

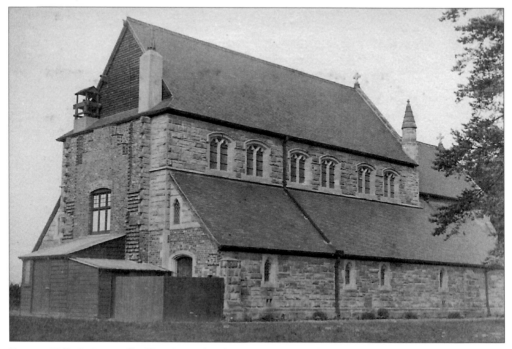

Turners Hill, St Leonard's Church south side, *c.* 1905. Its architect was Lacy W. Ridge, and it was consecrated in 1895. Judging by the roughness of the left-hand end, a tower was always intended to be added, and this was completed in 1923 to the design of Sir Aston Webb. The top of the tower is 575 ft above sea level.

Turners Hill Fire Brigade, *c.* 1940. It was formed in 1939. Front row, from left to right: Norman Billings, Tom Fieldwick, Eric Lake, Frank Rice, Major Vidler, Owen Skinner, Jimmy Wild. Back row: Noel Wells, Murdo McLeod, Les Budgen, Ern Constable, John Richardson, George Billings, Beau Simmons, Dick Lucas, Fred Peachey. (H. Connold)

Turners Hill, Withypitts Hill, looking south towards Selsfield and Haywards Heath. On the right-hand side of the road, beyond the pond in the centre of this view, is Withy Pits Farm. (Lowman's Photo Series)

Two girls outside the Red Lion, Lion Lane, Turners Hill. 'H. Holman' is the name on the inn sign (left), but dating the picture on this evidence presents difficulty as directories issued between 1895 and 1934 show Henry Holman as innkeeper for the whole of that time.

Turners Hill and Worth Village Band with a trophy, c. 1920. This band performed between the early 1900s and early 1950s. In the back row, from left to right: first, Albert Langridge; third, Nobby Bennett; fourth, George Wells; eighth, Bert Streeter. Middle row, third from left: Arty Denman. Front row, from left to right: first, George Webber; second, Horace Dawson; fourth, Mr Taylor; fifth, Harry Colbran; sixth, Oliver Wells; eighth, Henry Wells. Others have not been identified.

Church Parade at Turners Hill featuring the village band, boy scouts and even a policeman, 1910. The picture is believed to have been taken by Arthur Harding of East Grinstead.

The Grove, *c.* 1900. This rather exotic house stands ¼ mile south-west of Turners Hill, but since this photograph was taken the appearance of the house has been much altered. In particular, the battlements are gone and there is now a pitched roof.

WEST HOATHLY &
SHARPTHORNE

The Vinol's Cross Inn, between West Hoathly and Sharpthorne, with the road to Highbrook leading off to the south. In a porchway a woman in black keeps watch on the four boys and the photographer. This house now forms part of the inn, rebuilt with three dormers, and the doorway on the older part behind the boys has been bricked up. The row of cottages has been demolished.

The Cat Inn, West Hoathly, *c.* 1910. This unusually named public house dates back to the early sixteenth century with Victorian additions to the left. The house beyond the inn is called The Strakes. (Bond's Series)

North Lane, West Hoathly, *c.* 1920. On the left is Old Timbers; to the right is the village shop with its bow-tied proprietor standing in the doorway. This shop later became Maynard's butchers, but no longer functions, now being called Bowfield Cottage. Note the Ford delivery van in the yard.

North Lane, with Red House on the right; this exquisite front garden has since been replaced by a brick-paved forecourt. The forge at the end of the lane flourished until 1963, and the building itself was burned down in 1967. (Bond's Series)

A closer look at the forge at the north end of North Lane, looking south-east. Next to the forge is 'Cobwebbs'. The steep hill is named The Hollow and leads to Vinol's Cross and Sharpthorne. After the destruction of the forge by fire, Forge Cottage was built on its site. (Valentine)

Chapel Row, West Hoathly, looking south-east, *c.* 1910. Four children sit outside the wheelwright's premises, now called Potter's House, almost hidden behind the large tree (now gone). It all looks very rough; today there are neat kerbstones to mark the division between road and walkway. (Bond's Series)

The Priest House, West Hoathly, in ruinous condition some time before 1908. Built in the fifteenth century as an estate office for the monks of St Pancras, Lewes, it became a farmhouse in the sixteenth century. It is timber framed with a dwarf wall of sandstone, and since 1908 has been a museum, owned by the Sussex Archaeological Society from 1935.

A parade in Queen's Square by the Cat Inn, 5 September 1909. The large banner in the background is held by the Ancient Order of Foresters, a permanent benefit society. On the left is Combers Cottage. (A. Harding, East Grinstead)

Funeral procession in Queen's Square, seen from an upper room of the Cat, looking south in the early 1930s. On the right is Combers Cottage, next to it the parsonage and beyond that is glimpsed the boundary wall of the Manor House.

Open-air service being held at West Hoathly for the Jubilee of King George V, 12 May 1935. This is viewed from the top terrace of the churchyard, looking north-east. By the drums is a flag of the British Legion. (Hamiltons, Brighton)

W. Reynolds and his extensive family at their home, the Red House, North Lane, West Hoathly, c. 1900. Mr Reynolds was a local builder. (Carr & Hopperton, East Grinstead)

West Hoathly School girls' stoolball team, with Mr Hazeldene, in the 1920s. The game, which is similar to cricket, requires the use of paddle-shaped bats. In the back row of this group, second from the right, is the headmistress, Mrs Rothwell.

West Hoathly football team, during the 1952/3 season. Back row, left to right: Harold Willie, Joe Cave, John Willie, J. Hazeldine, Ted Howick, -?-, Mr Charlwood, Ray Parks, Tony Chapman and Harry Carter. Front row: Snowy Howick, Ivor Thomas, Fred Willie, John Cave and Len Barnard.

A barely recognizable Sharpthorne, east end looking west, in the early 1900s. On the left, obscured by the tree, are Sharpthorne Villas. On the right is Station Road and on the hill behind stands West Hoathly. (W. Page, East Grinstead)

Top Road, Sharpthorne. A shop – Francis's drapery – has now been built on the corner of Station Road. Later it became Taylor's Stores; Kingswood Stores from the mid-1950s to 1977; Mace Food Store from 1978 to 1987. At present it is Sharpthorne Stores, with an extension on the east side.

The Stoneland Players, Sharpthorne. This shows one of several Greek plays that were performed at Stonelands. Ursula Ridley, who was a noted historian of West Hoathly, stands in the centre. One hopes that the sheep on the left could act as well as the rest of the cast.

Sharpthorne, West Hoathly.   59.   Bond's Photo Series.

A trap in Top Road, Sharpthorne, west end looking east, *c.* 1910. The first cottage on the left in this picture has since been demolished; beyond it still stands Sharpthorne House, as does Railway Cottage on the right. (Bond's Series)

A. Barnard, Sharpthorne's village policeman, outside the police house in Sharpthorne, 1935. The high-buttoned tunic was abolished soon after the Second World War. The police house is now Old Autumn Cottage.

The class of Highbrook School, 11 May 1905. None of the girls in pinafores or boys in knickerbockers has been identified. On the left is a very young assistant teacher, and at the back, assuming an air of detachment and aloofness, can only be the headmistress. Highbrook, a hamlet 1¼ miles south-west of West Hoathly, boasts a remarkably fine church, a landmark easily seen from the Bluebell Railway. (Redhill Photo Co.)

ACKNOWLEDGEMENTS

I am grateful to the Trustees of East Grinstead Town Museum for making eighty-four photographs from its collection available for publication. Many of these were acquired in June 1996 and were formerly owned by the late Brian Desmond. Of the other pictures in this book, twenty-five were loaned by M.J. Leppard, one by Diana Harris and a further twenty-five were supplied from my own collection.

The following supplied much information and several photographs about their villages: Peter Bateman (Felbridge), four; Eric Byford (Forest Row), fifteen; Eric Dawes (Turners Hill), six; J.S. Hodgkinson (Crawley Down), eight; Arthur Hunt (Ashurst Wood), six; Mike Parcell (Hartfield), six; G. Steer (Lingfield and Dormansland), five; West Hoathly Local History Society (West Hoathly and Sharpthorne), seventeen.

Photographs are credited, where known, to their original publishers or photographers. Unfortunately several original prints, and most copy prints, do not carry these details and in most cases it is virtually impossible to ascertain them.

My thanks go to Michael Leppard (trustee of East Grinstead Town Museum), Dorothy Hatswell (its honorary curator) and Keith Brown (chairman of East Grinstead Museum Society) for the enormous assistance given to me in the compilation of this book.

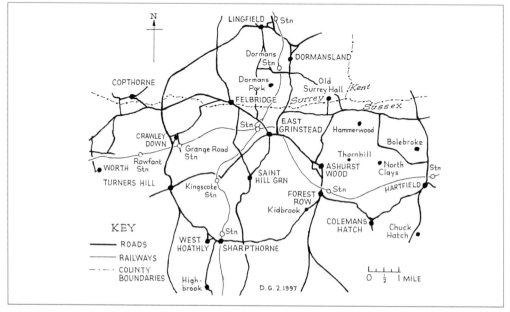

East Grinstead and surrounding area.

To order any of these titles please telephone our distributor, Littlehampton Book Services on 01903 7215
For a catalogue of these and our other titles please ring Regina Schinner on 01453 731114